Echoes Of The Soul

Reflections in Rhyme

Tahera Jadhav

Copyright © Tahera Jadhav
All Rights Reserved.

This book has been self-published with all reasonable efforts taken to make the material error-free by the author. No part of this book shall be used, reproduced in any manner whatsoever without written permission from the author, except in the case of brief quotations embodied in critical articles and reviews.

The Author of this book is solely responsible and liable for its content including but not limited to the views, representations, descriptions, statements, information, opinions, and references ["Content"]. The Content of this book shall not constitute or be construed or deemed to reflect the opinion or expression of the Publisher or Editor. Neither the Publisher nor Editor endorse or approve the Content of this book or guarantee the reliability, accuracy, or completeness of the Content published herein and do not make any representations or warranties of any kind, express or implied, including but not limited to the implied warranties of merchantability, fitness for a particular purpose.

The Publisher and Editor shall not be liable whatsoever...

Made with ❤ on the BookLeaf Publishing Platform
www.bookleafpub.in
www.bookleafpub.com

Dedication

To every heart that seeks beauty,
hope, and meaning in life's
moments—
may these poems resonate with
your soul and bring you light

Preface

Poetry is a mirror to the soul, reflecting our deepest emotions, thoughts, and dreams. Each poem in this book carries a piece of life's essence—some may move you to tears, others may bring a smile, but all are meant to inspire and connect.

Regret not if my poems make you sad,
For there will be many to make you glad.
Some may make you truly cry,
But many will fill your heart with joy.
With some, you might in horror recoil,
And some may even make your blood boil.
Some may stir passions and dreams,
While others will make your heart gleam.
With some, I may appear to tease,
But most will bring you love and peace.
These words are mere tidbits of our lives,
As each day, to do better, you and I strive.

Acknowledgements

With heartfelt gratitude, I acknowledge the All-Knowing, the All-Mighty, without whose Will no pen can move and no thought can take shape. Every word in this collection is inspired by His guidance and grace.

I extend my deepest appreciation to my parents and family, whose unwavering love, encouragement, and support have been my greatest strength. Their belief in me has been a source of constant motivation, and without them, this journey would not have been possible.

This book is a reflection of faith, hope, and the beauty of life's experiences. May these words inspire and uplift all who read them.

1. Before I go

Before my journey meets its end,
Before I round the final bend,
Before I bid the world goodbye,
Before I spread my wings and fly,

My heart longs deeply to convey
That all I am, this very day,
Is shaped by those along my way.

My deepest thanks to every soul
Who lit my path, who made me whole,
Who ran for me that extra mile,
And filled my days with love and smiles.

Grateful am I for hearts so true,
Who stood beside me, firm and few,
Through stormy tides and restless night,
Their presence shining, warm and bright.

How could I leave without a plea

For those I hurt unknowingly—
The ones I failed in time of need,
Or wounded through some
thoughtless deed?

Before I go, before we part,
I ask with pure and open heart—
Forgive my faults, forget my wrong,
And send me off with love and song.

2. Thy Love O God is A to Z

Thy love, O God
Assures Your presence,
Breathes life into our withered souls,
Caresses our broken wings,
Draws us to Thee.

Thy love, O God
Encompasses and embraces,
Flows to each soul,
Glows in each heart,
Heals the deepest wounds.

Thy love, O God
Is infinite,
Joins hearts in unity,
Kindles the flame of service,
Leads the way.

Thy love, O God
Mends shattered lives,

Nourishes and nurtures,
Opens hearts to understanding,
Purifies and purges.

Thy love, O God
Quickens the spirit,
Revives the dead,
Shelters the weary,
Tends to every need.

Thy love, O God
Understands our deepest longings,
Values the smallest acts of devotion,
Washes away despair,
EXalts the humble and meek.

Thy love, O God
Yields blessings beyond measure,
Zephyr's peace into troubled souls.

3. Enable us to serve

Enable us to serve, O Lord
Without longing for praise,
Without fear of disappointment,
Without hope for reward,
Without desire for rest.

Enable us to serve, O Lord
With the devotion of a martyr,
With the passion of a lover,
With the innocence of a child,
With the courage of a warrior.

Enable us to serve, O Lord
As a humble drop in the ocean,
As a radiant star in the sky,
As a gentle, refreshing breeze,
As the Beloved Master served,
Until our final breath.

4. Thrill

If the road isn't bumpy,
If the path is all clear,
What thrill would there be
When the destination draws near?

If the night isn't pitch dark,
If the clouds don't cast their shroud,
What thrill would there be
When the sunrise breaks the cloud?

If the waves aren't soaring,
If the lightning strikes not with might,
What thrill would there be
When the shore is in sight?

If you don't sweat day and night,
If you're not tired down to the bone,
What thrill would there be
When you've fought all on your own?

5. Thy Gifts, my submissions

What can I call my own?
My land, my wealth, my beautiful home.

What belongs to me?
My children, my parents, my sweet family.

All that I possess:
My name, my fame, my worldly success.

All my belongings and all that exists,
These are not mine,
These are Thy gifts.

All is Yours, and as a trust, I keep.
If You wish to recall them,
Why should I weep?

You know the beginning, You know the end,
You know what to give,
And when to send.

My sight is limited, Your vision I can't perceive.
Give me both the courage to let go,
And with gratitude to receive.

Enable me to submit, Thy will to accept,
Thou hast power over all things,
Thou knows what is best.

I love what you ordain, I love what you behest.
Bestow your grace,
Protect me from tests.

If it be Your will to grant, if you decree,
Your blessings will descend,
No power can deter Thee.

6. Embracing the journey

No man is perfect;
We all make blunders.
We bask in the rain,
But must face the thunder.

It's our destiny to stumble and stand,
How can we not slip?
When we have to walk on sand.

The journey would be dull,
On a straight, easy road.
Our inner strength shines,
Only when we shoulder the load.

We can either fall and weep,
Or brave the climb—dangerous and steep.
We might grumble and regret,
But can we be grateful, yet upset?

Let's embrace it as an adventure;

Let's stride forward with pride.
He illuminates our path—
He is our Guide.

7. Stay True

Life is a complicated mystery,
Much like a maze.
It has so many crossroads,
Feels like wandering in a haze.

There are times you want to run,
But you must gracefully stop.
And when you want to rest,
You will be forced into a painful hop.

The turns and twists are sudden,
They appear out of the blue.
And if you want to make it,
You should know how to be true.

If you're true to yourself,
The way will be clear.
But if others cloud your actions,
Your heart will always be in fear.

If you're true to your journey,
It will let you learn and lead.
But if you just want to reach the end,
You will keep falling off your steed.

It takes courage to traverse the ups and downs,
And humility to learn what went wrong.
It takes resilience to keep your flame strong,
And optimism to hum a grateful song.

The journey takes every bit and atom of you,
But it will transform and make you new.
Don't worry, you will pass through,
Just stay true, just stay true.

8. Faith's Flame

When the nether world seems like a dust heap,
And His love in your blood flows.
When you are oblivious to existence,
That's when true Faith grows.

When you live on this mortal plane,
But your soul roams in the realms on high.
When His love throbs in your heart,
Then no pain can make you sigh.

When, like unto gold,
You are thrown into fire.
When the heat makes you glow,
That's when you're released from desire.

When the moth mingles with the flame,
And the athirst drinks deep from the spring.
When the longing one beholds the Beloved,

That's when your soul begins to sing.

When you seek only His good pleasure,
When you desire only His face.
When you tread only on His path,
That's when you receive Eternal Grace.

9. Eternal Joy

Prostrating at Thy Holy Threshold,
Submitting completely to Thy Will,
My heart beats frantically,
Yet my soul is still.

Communing only with Thee,
Baring my thoughts,
Revealing each secret,
Yet my speech is lost.

Setting sight on Thy Mercy,
Gazing besottedly above,
Looking at Thy Heaven,
With tears of love.

Hearkening to Thy Call,
Listening to Thy voice,
Thy melodies ringing in the air,
As my ears rejoice.

As I turn to Thee, O God,
My whole being is renewed,
All else vanishes,
As with eternal joy I am imbued.

10. Meeting Death

Death will kiss one day,
And embrace the body to dust.
This worldly play will end,
For the fall of the curtains is a must.

Death will greet us one day,
Guiding us to her fold.
Our breaths shall cease,
As her beauty we behold.

Death will walk in with hushed steps,
And whisper in soft tones.
She will bid us to follow
Leaving all that we own.

But death will also open the door,
For a journey bright.
The soul will fly to its Creator,
To the Kingdom of light.

Death will break the cage asunder,
And the bird will be set free
The soul will rush to its Beloved,
To the Realm of True Reality.

Death will come,
As a messenger of joy.
She will bring gifts of peace,
Which for eternity we shall enjoy.

11. Love

Love is endless,
Love is deep,
Love is eternal,
And forever to keep.

Love nurtures,
Love guides ,
Love protects,
But it can never hide.

Love multiplies ,
Love grows,
Love blossoms ,
When care one shows.

Love is precious,
Love is kind,
Love understands,
But is hard to find.

Where there is love
Angels abound,
Blessed is the one,
In whose heart such love is found.

12. Finding joy

If you are unhappy or sad,
If you are angry and mad,
If your heart is not at rest,
If your life is void of zest,

If your grief you can't comprehend,
And your troubles don't seem to end,
Then reach out to those in need,
Perform with love some selfless deed,
Bring a smile and wipe someone's tears,
Give them love and send them prayers,
Give your strength to someone weak,
Share your courage with those who seek,
Then your sorrow will melt away,
Joy to your heart will find its way,
The cheer that you spread will envelop you,
And to your sadness you
will bid adieu.

13. Trust

When there is darkness all around
And not a flicker in sight,
Yet I trust that at the end of the tunnel,
There will be abundant light.

When the land is all dry
And not a single flower in sight,
Yet I trust that the rains will fall,
And the gardens will bloom in delight.

When there is silence all around,
And not a syllable or sound,
Yet I trust that the harp will be found,
And songs of joy will abound.

What is this trust,
That keeps our hopes so high?
That keeps us going,
When others grieve or sigh.

To trust is to submit
Without question or doubt.
To trust is to believe
In God's wisdom throughout.

To trust does not mean
That you don't try your best.
It means that you do your part

And to God leave the rest.

14. Life's Pages

We are all writing a book,
The book of our life.
And each day a new page we inscribe.

Some pages smell of hardwork and sweat.
Some pages with tears of agony are wet.

Some pages shine with success and joy,
Some pages we will always enjoy.

Some pages are all wreathed in smiles,
Some pages make our struggles worthwhile.

Some pages make us rebound in fear,
Some pages have blotches of difficulties here and there.

Some pages we wish to forever erase,
Some pages are hidden in disgrace.

Some pages make us laugh out wild,

Some pages are filled with anecdotes wise.

Some pages make us happy and proud,
Some pages make us cry out loud.

Some pages scream with deceit and lies,
Some pages fill us with surprise.

Some pages our patience show,
Some pages with golden ink glow.

Some pages are perfumed with love and care,
Some pages are precious and rare.

Let us pen this book in such wise
That will inspire others to overcome and rise.

We will all reach its last page one day,
May it be worthy to be read and show others the way .

15. The Power of Words

Words of encouragement,
Words of true praise,
Words woven in love ,
Our confidence they raise.

Words of enthusiasm,
Words of zest,
Words woven in joy,
Bring out our best.

Words of assurance,
Words of relief,
Words woven in trust,
Make us believe .

Words can caress,
Words can heal,
Words are precious,
Their power we can feel.

16. Gratitude

It is easy to be thankful
When you get what you desire,
But to constantly look for good
Even when the situation is dire,
That is gratitude.

If you can bring thankfulness
Into all that takes place,
Rather than keep waiting
For your sorrows to erase,
That is gratitude.

If simple things you enjoy
And small joys you relish,
If you don't take things for granted,
And if every memory you cherish,
That is gratitude.

That which turns chaos into order,
Confusion into clarity,

Denial into acceptance,
Discord into solidarity,
That is gratitude.

That which turns a house into a home,
And a meal into a feast,
Tests into rewards,
And troubles to ease,
That is gratitude.

That which unlocks
The fullness of life and its purpose,
And turns what we have
Into enough and surplus,
That is gratitude.

That which makes sense of our past,
Brings peace for today,
Creates vision for tomorrow
And gives courage to hold on and pray,
That is gratitude.

17. His Name

His Name on my lips,
Every morn , every night.
His Name in my heart,
Through darkness, through light.

His Name in my thoughts,
Every moment, every day.
His Name in my prayers,
At every crossroad along the way.

His Name in my sorrows,
In my anguish, in my fears.
His Name in my solitude,
Through my smiles, through my tears.

His Name in my joys,
In my laughter, in my delight.
His Name in my smiles
Each dawn, each midnight.

His Name in my being ,
In my tests, in my woes.
His Name in my soul,
At work or in repose.

His Name my balm, His Name my relief,
His Name my trust, His Name my belief,
His Name my love, His Name my friend,
His Name my origin, His Name my end.

18. You

The passion that grips your being,
So intense, so strong,
The purpose of your existence,
The goal for which your soul longs.

The pursuit that captivates you,
The dream that rages fire,
The aspirations that you chase,
That drives your heart's desire.

The fuel that keeps you going,
And pumps your zeal,
The inspiration that keeps coming,
And all your pain that heals.

The labour that requires perseverance,
Yet never lets you tire,
The mission that demands sacrifice,
Yet makes you fly higher.

The task that consumes your self,
But reveals the true YOU.
That's your essence,
And that's what you should DO.

19. God's Blessings

I sat under the shade of God's tree
And gasped in delight as
The breeze of His love stirred me up,
The fruits of His knowledge quenched my hunger,
The canopy of His leaves
sheltered me from blazing tests,
The fragrance of His flowers
awakened my inner being,
The dew drops refreshed
my drooping soul,
And the song of the birds gave joyful tidings.
And then under His Graceful Abundant shade,
Seeds of gratitude, of happiness,
of humilty, of hope ,
of strength, of eternal love,
Were gently sowed in the soil of my heart
And a new life began to unfold
A life where each breath pulsates
To the rhythm of only His name.

20. God's Favourite Colour

Which colour is God's favourite?
Is it the green of the trees?
Or the red of the roses,
Or the blue of the seas ?

Does He love the brown soil more?
Or the black of the night?
Or Is it the orange hue of sunsise?
Or the clouds that shine white?

He who is the Fashioner of every colour,
Loves the colour of a soul pure.
He loves the colour of unity,
The colour, that binds the world whole.

He loves the colour of joy,
The colour of peace,
May my heart be dyed in the colour of His love,
A love that will never cease.

21. Like a ....

Like a sunflower,
That Turns to the sun,
I turn my heart to you , O my Beloved!

Like a river,
That falls into the ocean,
I surrender myself to you , O my Lord!

Like a leaf,
That moves with the wind,
I rejoice in Thy will , O my Master!

Like the soil,
That thirsts for the rain,
My soul yearns for Thy blessings, O my God!

Like a bird,
That flies towards the horizon,
My prayers hasten to Thy throne, O my King!

Like the waves,
That wash the ocean shore,
My heart is cleansed of all desires but Thee , O my
Creator!

Everything in nature,
Bows in gratitude to Thee,
And celebrates Thy praise.

Make my soul
To be like the sunflower, the river, the leaves,
the soil, the bird , the waves.

Accept our humble deeds, accept our servitude
Make us firm in Thy path ,
Shower on us Thy love and certitude.

22. Submission to Thee

When I lay my head on the ground
And utter Thy praise,
And express my gratitude,
And tell You of my fears,
And confide in You my wishes,
And beg Thee for forgiveness,
And yearn for Thy love.

Then in those magical moments, I feel
The power of Thy Majesty,
The warmth of Thy Nearness,
The touch of Thy Healing,
The sweetness of Thy Bounty,
The assurance of Thy Assistance,
The safety of Thy Protection.

What mystery Thou hast concealed, O God!
In this act of prayer and submission!
What Mercy Thou hast revealed!

May you accept our soul's murmurs
For only to Thee it bows and kneels.

23. Drop by drop

A drop of kindness,
A drop of a smile,
A drop of an encouraging nod,
Each drop is worthwhile.

A drop of empathy,
A drop of care,
A drop of forgiveness,
Each drop is a prayer.

A drop of compassion,
A drop of respect,
A drop of generosity,
Each drop has an effect.

A drop of hope,
A drop of gratitude,
A drop of love,
Each drop has magnitude.

A drop of joy,
A drop of humility,
A drop of a moment,
Each drop brings tranquility.

Drop by drop
His bounties pour.
Drop by drop,
Blessings galore.

24. Prayer

As I sit down in solitude,
And bow down my head in prayer,
I open my heart to my Creator,
To the One who is All Aware.

I lay my troubles,
And all my affairs,
I lay my concerns,
And all my fears.

I beg for His guidance,
I seek His grace.
I yearn for His love,
And His assuring embrace.

I lay my follies,
And all my mistakes.
I lay my shortcomings,
And all my heartaches.

I beg for His mercy,
And seek His compassionate gaze,
I yearn for His forgiveness,
And He never fails to amaze.

He erases all sorrows,
And replaces darkness with light.
He opens new doors,
And fills my heart with delight.

With each prayer that is uttered,
The turmoils in my soul cease,
My griefs fade away,
And I am filled with peace.

Now only gratitude flows,
And all else in its force dissolves.
I gird up for His service, He around whom my life
revolves,
With a firm resolve ! With a firm resolve!

25. Fleeting Moments

In a fleeting moment, how things can change,
It all depends on what God ordains.
Kings to beggars,
And mountains to plains.
Sorrows to happiness,
And droughts to rains.

In a fleeting moment, how things can change,
It all depends on what God ordains.
Prosperity to hunger,
And respect to disdain.
Life to death,
And freedom to chains.

In a fleeting moment, how things can change,
It all depends on what God ordains.
Doubt to conviction,
And loss to gains.
Hatred to love,
And contentment to complaints.

In a fleeting moment, how things can change,
It all depends on what God ordains.
Darkness to light,
And shame to fame.
Crowds to isolation,
And joy to pain.

So live in the moment and give some thought,
What's our life's purpose and how should it be sought?
What path should we tread and why this plight?
Let sow in our hearts some wisdom and insight.

26. God-An Eternal Friend

A love that can be felt at all times,
A love for which my heart pines,
A deep feeling of belongingness,
In Whose presence, I am but nothingness.

Who is This Eternal Friend of mine?
Whose name in my heart, day and night, shines.
Who wipes my tears and makes me smile,
Who makes my life worthwhile.

A Friend before Whom my soul bows,
The secrets of my heart He alone knows.

27. Victorious Men

Men who conquer mountains,
Men who ride the waves,
Men who tame the tempests,
Men who are strong and brave.

Men who reach the summit,
Men who win the seas,
Men who love challenges,
Men who never cease!

What makes these men victorious
And their lives so legendary?
What makes them so fearless
And their attitude so visionary?

What makes them so glorious,
Do you want to know?
They dream and they believe,
And their inner light glows.

They have a deep faith,
That no one can shake,
They work hard and persevere
And their hopes can never break.

28. Beloved to Beloved

This life is bestowed by my Lord,
I came into this world of His accord,
but the trappings here, caught my feet
I almost forgot that Him again, I would meet.
He sent me to realise my innate potential,
For that, challenges are so essential
But somewhere on the way I forgot,
That His help is what I should have sought.
He is my Beloved, watching over me,
Waiting for me to reach my destiny,
But the glitters and dazzles got me drowned,
I forgot that His love always abounds.
He is my Beginning, He is my end,
He is the source on which my life depends.
Beloved to Beloved is the story of each soul,
Let's remember that He is our ultimate goal.

29. The Tree of Faith

The tree of Faith,
Doesn't grow in haste.
The cup of sacrifice, if you're willing to taste,
And afflictions on His path, you're eager to face,
If for tests and trials your heart longs,
And whatever maybe, you're steadfast and strong,
If even riches and wealth fail to entice,
And your heart is pure and free of prejudice,
Then Faith will blossom and your heart will glow,
And the love of God through you will flow.

30. Death-A Messenger of Joy

When my voice you can no longer hear.

And my touch is nowhere near,

When in eternal sleep my eyes close,

And on my grave you have laid your rose,

Don't get lost in the maze of grief,

Don't let sorrow descend and weep.

This body is mortal, it was bound to die,

But the soul is eternal, to its Creator it will fly.

This body was only a temporal abode,

My identity was and is my soul.

The love and laughter, the sun and shade,

Don't worry, will never ever fade.

Memories are woven into our souls,

Unlike the body, they don't get old.

There is so much ecstasy in the soul's flight,

There is love and peace and wonderful light.

Reunion with God is our goal,

God welcomes us into His loving fold.

Death, our soul cannot destroy,

It's a messenger of everlasting life and joy,
Death is not some tragic end,
It's the beginning of a new journey with God,
our immortal friend.

31. The Journey Within

The journey was tough,
The roads were rough,
The valleys steep,
The oceans deep,
Steps were heavy and the eyes wept,
The sun of hope was about to set.
But then a tiny voice sang,
"Don't give up," these words rang,
"Lofty missions are not achieved in play,
You have to toil, every day,
Enjoy the beauty while on the way,
Every blade of grass has something to say,
Don't be afraid to falter and fall,
Unraveling life's purpose is your quest after all."
Prayers lovingly held my hands,
And faith enabled me to stand.
Courage smiled and came by my side,
With renewed zeal, I resumed my stride.

32. Love and Peace

How many blasts will deafen our ears,
Before we realize,
That love and peace have a sound so sweet,
And in war, it's only a revengeful beat.

How much smoke will obstruct our eyes,
Before we realize,
That love and peace give us a vision,
And eyes blinded with war can't envision.

How many horrid screams will dry up our throats,
Before we realize,
That songs of progress sung in love and peace,
In war, are just sorrowful mourns.

How many limbs will cease to move,
Before we realize,
That love and peace motivate worthy deeds,
And in war, it's only hatred and greed.

How many gallons of blood will we shed,
Before we realize,
That love can turn a foe into a friend,
And in war, even brothers hunger for each other's end.

How much hunger will we bear,
Before we realize,
That prosperity which thrives in love and peace,
In war, just withers away.

How many souls will wing their flight,
Before we realize,
The ecstasy of a soul in love and peace,
And its agony in warring plight.

How many more wars will torment the human race?
When will wars be finally wiped off earth's beautiful
face?
How many more wars will we fight,
Before it's too late to even realize.

33. Touch

The touch of my father
So gentle, so sweet
His kiss on my forehead
His caress on my cheek
It doesn't matter how old I may grow
I still cherish his touch wherever I go.
No matter how many miles apart
I'll always be his daughter, the princess of his heart.

The touch of my brother
So protecting, so strong
His hugs and pats say it all
He'll always be there, no matter how much we brawl.
Our care for each other will never cease
I'll always be his sister and our love will never decrease.

The touch of my lover
So intoxicating, so profound
It's trust, it's faith, it has our souls bound.
Many ups and downs in life we'll share

Our love is to be nurtured every day with care
No matter how many turns and twists
Our love is eternal, it will always exist.

The touch of my friends
So secure and safe
So understanding and full of grace
An assuring handshake, a nod that knows
How to make me smile in my woes
I'll always be his friend and he'll stand by my side
There's a mutual respect within which we abide.

The touch of a stranger
That can touch even through eyes
His intentions so disgusting, his laugh so vile
The shameless hunger that makes him a beast
He attacks my essence with his wildness unleashed

When will these soul-less creatures be punished?
When will their touch be reviled and admonished?
How long will justice be denied?
How long will my pride be defiled?

34. A worthy life

These eyes that relish nature's beauty
May they also seek the goodness in each soul.
These ears that hear such beautiful melodies
May they also hearken to Thy wondrous tones.
This nose that inhales the fragrance of flowers
May it also breathe in the attar from above.
These hands that create such outstanding marvels
May they also serve others with true love.
These feet that tread to so many destinations
May they walk on the path that is Thine
This heart that is full of worldly desires
May it be sanctified and shine.
This tongue that can speak a myriad languages
May it glorify and sing Thy praise
This life that Thou hast gifted
May with Your love glow and be ablaze.

35. Living my life on my own terms

If on my own terms, I live my life,
There'd only be love, no worthless strife.
Joy and happiness would always abound
There'd always be a smile to pass around.
Hearts would be pure and kind,
The purpose would be to serve mankind.
There'd always be a heart willing to listen
Faces with joy would shine and glisten.
There'd always be a helping hand
No obstacles that together, we can't withstand.
Laughter would make our days bright
And in gratitude, we would pray at night.
Life would have a beautiful meaning
Each new day, radiant and appealing.
So when time comes to wing our way
"I'm proud of you," even God would say.

36. Be the love

Be the love that you never received,
Be the heart that never deceived,
Be the friend that never left your side,
Be the light that never failed to guide.
Be the words that you longed to hear,
Be the peace that was so dear,
Be the ocean that never dries,
Be the sun that never fails to rise.
Be the smile that you longed to see,
Be the shade of a beautiful tree,
Be the hand that you wished to hold,
Be the face of the one you longed to behold.

37. Forgiveness

Someone's words may be curt,
Or someone's behaviour may badly hurt,
In anguish you may lament and weep,
For your heart is wounded very deep.

If you want your heart to truly heal,
And your grief forever to seal,
Then forgive the one who has wronged,
You will be gifted with the peace you so longed.

38. Hold On

A tiny seed struggled
Alone in the dark.
Ready to sacrifice itself,
Did it know, from it, a tree would spark?
Don't be overwhelmed by calamities,
That have come your way.
The night is about to end,
And the sun is on its way.
If thorns prick your feet,
And ordeals deepen your wounds and make you bleed,
Then stand more firm and staunch in His path,
Hold the cord of patience and fasten your grasp.
Rely on His blessings, His abounding grace.

39. Waking up early

I love to wake up early,
To see the sun rise.
Its victory over darkness,
To witness with my eyes.

I love to wake up early,
To see the birds fly,
The joy in their wings,
As they conquer the sky.

I love to wake up early,
To feel the cool breeze,
Its caress on my cheeks,
As it turns troubles into ease.

I love to wake up early,
To see the flowers bloom,
Their petals as they open,
Wipe away all gloom.

I love to wake up early,
To thank God with my heart,
A new day has been gifted,
And I want to make a beautiful start.

40. Tears

Tears that secretly fill our eyes,
What emotions they wish to show or hide?
Oh! they are of so many types!
So hard to judge! So hard to describe!

Tears that glide in happiness,
When joy renders us speechless.
Tears that roll in loss and pain,
When love is ruined by disdain.

Tears that flow in separation,
For lost dreams and aspirations,
Tears that haunt us with our past,
Or flash from our eyes when aghast.

Tears that jump in surprise,
When broken hopes or ties revive.
Tears in repentance or loneliness,
Tears of anger or helplessness.

Tears shed in another's woes,
Tears for the love of God that flows,
All tears have a story untold,
A mystery for us to slowly unfold.

41. The Outward Trappings

As we traverse this earthy life,
Let's protect our souls from worthless strife.
These outward trappings of wealth and fame,
These vanities and craze for name,
All will vanish on this material plane,
When with death, we lose our mortal frame.
False pride and shameful deeds,
Powerful armies, lust and greed,
Entangle not your souls in them,
Waste not your precious lives on them,
Into dust they will finally be confined,
How can we be so dumb and blind?
Those with true knowledge and insight,
Turn their hearts to God's Eternal light,
Fully detached and full of His love,
They are showered with blessings from Heavens above.

42. Colour

The orange hues of sunrise,
The pure white snow,
The silky brown sands of the deserts,
Their beauty, do we really know?
The reds of the roses, the blues of the seas,
The lush green grass and the awesome trees,
God painted colours in all shades and blooms,
To dispel all monotony and to banish all gloom.
Richness in colours,
Enhance the vibrance all around.
If there was just one colour,
Would such beauty abound?
The beautiful diversity in the human race,
Various skin tones magnify our grace.
All of us in a unique complexion and design,
Handmade by our Creator, Wonderful and Divine.
Our skin may be black like the vast night sky,
Or white like the moon that shines on high.
It may be brown like the mountains steep,
Or have a tinge of yellow, a little light or slightly deep.

Whatever our skin colour,
We are all the same.
We all have a heart,
That beats in His name.
We are one, whatever our colour and race,
Towards God, let's turn our face.
The light of unity let us spread,
On the path of peace, let our feet tread.

43. God's Signature

The green fields were rolling by,
The clouds were smiling in the sky.
The river was slowly finding its way,
The birds were enjoying the blissful day.

The breeze was singing a lovely song,
The trees were waving all along.
The mountains afar seemed to dance,
And the sun cast a playful glance.

I marveled at this beautiful sight,
So evident is God's Majesty and Might.
His signature is all over the place—
His Beauty, His Power, His Wonderful Grace.

44. Life – A Beautiful Journey

We are all trekking a beautiful mountain,
At some places narrow and steep,
And each year we move closer
To its lofty, glorious peak.

On the way, we come across
Colorful flowers and waterfalls.
We cross valleys deep with sharp turns,
And occasionally, we may slip or fall.

But the mountain summit beckons us,
And all our tiredness fades.
Each year, we make new memories
As we move through sun and shade.

We meet fellow travelers on the way,
All trying to move up each day.
We smile and lend a helping hand,
And lift the fallen and make them stand.

Each year, there are victories and milestones crossed.
At each step, God's blessings and love are sought.
There are new challenges and some battles lost,
But He is always foremost in our thoughts.

If we celebrate each stride we take,
Thank God for all the leaps we make,
Then this journey becomes a memorable song—
We enjoy whatever comes along.

45. Tests and Trials

I saw a challenge coming my way,
I welcomed it and asked it to stay.
"Make me strong and brave," I said.
"On the path of courage, make me tread."

Some tests and trials knocked my door,
I invited them in, for I was sure
That they were blessings in disguise,
Who had come to make me more
Detached and wise.

A few sufferings became my friends,
They made me realize on what
True happiness depends.
Illnesses, losses, agonies, and pains—
A spiritual gift they contain.

The physical world is not the finality,
For our soul is an eternal reality.

All hardships let us with joy embrace,
And radiance always shines on our face.

46. Happiness

Oh! Don't say I have no happiness inside,
There's a treasure of smiles I cannot hide.

Just tickle me, and you will hear,
My sweet laughter ringing clear.

Happiness doesn't come from wealth or fame,
Chase them if you like, but you'll remain the same.

Happiness blooms when you make others smile,
When you forget your sorrows and make life
worthwhile.

Happiness grows when you bring others joy,
When you leave behind grief and simply enjoy.

The key to happiness lies in your hands,
Like a gift at your command.

47. Life

As we move on life's road,
Many milestones do we cross,
But there are always some puddles and pools,
And we seem at loss.

But then we learn how to overcome,
We change, we adapt, new tunes we hum.
Big boulders we move, and battles survive,
As we flip through the pages of our journey called life.

At times we get tired and have to stop,
We need some rest, to ponder and give thought,
But again, we bounce back with energy new,
Life beckons us with exciting hues.

We travel through the storms and the rains,
There are some losses, there are some gains.
We pick some flowers, we may fall in the dirt,
Sometimes we find joy, sometimes we get hurt.

Some arrive early, some arrive late,
But we all ultimately reach life's last gate,
The gate through which we finally enter our home,
To live in bliss under God's eternal dome.

48. Journey to Eternal Delight

When the time comes,
For my soul to say goodbye,
Like a dove to its nest,
It will joyfully fly.

When the time comes,
For my soul to say adieu,
Like a river it will rush
And into the ocean fall through.

When the time comes,
For my soul to bid farewell,
It will hasten to God,
And in His presence will dwell.

All life's sorrows and all life's sufferings
Will finally diffuse in His glorious light.
There'll only be love—pure and comforting,
To fill my soul with eternal delight.

49. Rely Upon God

These testing times will pass away,
Rely upon God, rejoice, and pray.

These are the times to detach ourselves,
To prove to God that we love Him above all else.

We need to reflect on why this crisis was born,
But also remember that there will be another dawn.

Our beautiful planet needs to heal,
With love and unity, this calamity we can deal.

We may lock the doors of our material rooms,
But can't we open our hearts' windows and dispel all the
gloom?

With illumined faces and radiant hearts,
Let's wait patiently and play our part.

50. True Beauty

True beauty lies in the soul,
It's my virtues that make me whole.

Lips that sing God's praise,
Are the most beautiful in this age.

Eyes that seek the goodness in each,
Their beauty is unique.

Hands that arise in servitude and prayer,
Aren't they the most precious, my dear?

Feet that tread the honest path,
What greater beauty is there to ask?

No matter how fat or small,
No matter how thin or tall,
No matter my height,
No matter if my hair is white,
No matter how many crooked teeth—

Physical beauty is just skin deep.

True beauty lies in the soul,
It's my virtues that make me whole.

51. Nature

Oh! Look at the mountains, the pines, the streams,
The soft grass, the clouds, the beautiful creeks.
Oh! Nature is such a wonderful treasure,
God must have made it in His leisure.

Oh! Look at the forests, the maples, the rivers,
The marshes, the rain, the thick green cover.
Oh! Nature is such a wonderful treasure,
God must have made it in His leisure.

Oh! Look at the deserts, the sands, the dunes,
The camels, the sun, the bright, glowing moon.
Oh! Nature is such a wonderful treasure,
God must have made it in His leisure.

Nature reflects the qualities of the Divine,
An expression of His will so sublime.
Oh! Nature is such a wonderful treasure,

52. Complement, Not Compete

I don't wish you to bow before me;
I am not a goddess to venerate.
But the respect that I cherish for you in my heart—
Wouldn't it be fair to receive an equal part?

I don't wish you to praise me day and night;
I am not a flawless diva with eternal youth.
But the way I love you beyond this flesh—
Can you not admire my beauty within?

I don't wish for you to always follow my footsteps;
I am not a leader born to guide.
But I long to walk the path of life
As a true friend, always by your side.

I don't wish for you to be my armored knight;
I, too, am a warrior, and my battles I can face and fight.
All I wish is that you stand by me
When times are not so right.

I want you to be with me.
Together, we walk step by step,
Holding hands and helping each other,
Sharing hope, courage, and zest.

We were meant to complement each other,
Not to compete.
We were meant to be counterparts,
Not to defeat.

When we abide in perfect love,
Manifold blessings descend from above.
The bird of humanity ascends to new heights,
Dispelling darkness and spreading light.

53. Equal I Am

Equal I am, equal I have always been.
The soul enlightening your being burns in me with the
same sheen.
Sown within us are the same seeds
Of noble thoughts, virtues, and deeds.
Equal I am, equal I have always been.

But alas! Ignorance set up a stage,
Spanning years and years of disgrace.
Exploitation and force ruled the show,
But now it's time the world should know
That equality cannot be fettered and chained—
Like the phoenix, it will soar again.

When this realization dawns true and clear,
When mutual respect erases all fear,
When education and opportunity are equal for all,
Peace and progress will never stall.
The bird of humanity will finally fly—
With both wings strong, we'll touch the sky.

www.ingramcontent.com/pod-product-compliance
Lightning Source LLC
Chambersburg PA
CBHW061701130726
47996CB00006B/2107